Mysteries in History
OAK ISLAND MYSTERY

by Katie Chanez

Ideas for Parents and Teachers

Pogo Books let children practice reading informational text while introducing them to nonfiction features such as headings, labels, sidebars, maps, and diagrams, as well as a table of contents, glossary, and index.

Carefully leveled text with a strong photo match offers early fluent readers the support they need to succeed.

Before Reading

- "Walk" through the book and point out the various nonfiction features. Ask the student what purpose each feature serves.
- Look at the glossary together. Read and discuss the words.

During Reading

- Have the child read the book independently.
- Invite them to list questions that arise from reading.

After Reading

- Discuss the child's questions. Talk about how they might find answers to those questions.
- Prompt the child to think more. Ask: Do you believe there is treasure on Oak Island? Why or why not?

Pogo Books are published by Jump!
3500 American Blvd W, Suite 150
Bloomington, MN 55431
www.jumplibrary.com

Copyright © 2026 Jump!
International copyright reserved in all countries. No part of this book may be reproduced in any form without written permission from the publisher.

Jump! is a division of FlutterBee Education Group.

Library of Congress Cataloging-in-Publication Data

Names: Chanez, Katie, author.
Title: Oak island mystery / Katie Chanez.
Description: Minneapolis, MN: Jump!, Inc., [2026]
Includes index.
Audience: Ages 7-10
Identifiers: LCCN 2025001511 (print)
LCCN 2025001512 (ebook)
ISBN 9798892138017 (hardcover)
ISBN 9798892138024 (paperback)
ISBN 9798892138031 (ebook)
Subjects: LCSH: History–Juvenile literature
Juvenile literature
Classification: LCC F1039.O35 C49 2026 (print)
LCC F1039.O35 (ebook)
DDC 971.1/28–dc23/eng/20250305
LC record available at https://lccn.loc.gov/2025001511
LC ebook record available at https://lccn.loc.gov/2025001512

Editor: Alyssa Sorenson
Designer: Molly Ballanger

Photo Credits: Uvgreen/Shutterstock, cover (shovel); 2happy/Shutterstock, cover (paper); Pyty/Shutterstock, cover (map); Adwo/Adobe Stock, 1; serikbaib/Adobe Stock, 3; mozZz/Adobe Stock, 4; S. Vincent/Shutterstock, 5; Nova Scotia Archives, 6-7, 10-11; grey_and/Shutterstock, 8 (left); Shamils/Shutterstock, 8 (right); chittakorn59/Shutterstock, 9 (stone); maradon 333/Shutterstock, 9 (background); Richard McCully/Wikimedia, 12-13; Timothy Kuratek/CBS Photo Archive/Getty, 14-15; francisblack/iStock, 15; Eduardo Estellez/Shutterstock, 16; Historical Picture Archive/Corbis/Getty, 16-17; Stillgravity/Shutterstock, 18; Hihitetlin/Shutterstock, 19 (inset); mark higgins/Shutterstock, 19; Paul Andreassen/Alamy, 20-21; Anton-Burakov/Shutterstock, 23.

Printed in the United States of America at Corporate Graphics in North Mankato, Minnesota.

TABLE OF CONTENTS

CHAPTER 1
A Mysterious Island 4

CHAPTER 2
Treasure Hunt 8

CHAPTER 3
Other Theories 18

QUICK FACTS & TOOLS
Map and Quick Facts 22
Glossary 23
Index 24
To Learn More 24

CHAPTER 1

A MYSTERIOUS ISLAND

Oak Island is off the coast of Nova Scotia, Canada. In 1795, Daniel McGinnis wanted to **explore**.

He rowed a boat to Oak Island. While in the woods, he found a large oak tree with a branch sawed off. Nobody lived on the island. So who did it? Why? There was a dip in the dirt. Was the branch pointing to it?

Oak Island

CHAPTER 1 5

The next day, he brought friends. They began to dig. They made a hole about 13 feet (4.0 meters) wide. They started digging down. About two feet (0.6 m) down, they found a **layer** of rocks. But they were not from the island. How did they get here?

They kept digging. About 10 feet (3.0 m) down, they found a wooden **platform**. There were more farther down. What else was buried here?

WHAT DO YOU THINK?

Have you ever found anything while exploring? What was it?

CHAPTER 1 7

CHAPTER 2
TREASURE HUNT

In 1804, a company paid men to dig the same hole. They found more platforms 90 feet (27 m) down. They found coconut **fibers**, too. Coconuts grow more than 1,000 miles (1,600 kilometers) away! How did they get on Oak Island?

fibers

They also found a stone. It had strange markings on it. Some people believed they were a **code**. They think it said, "Forty feet below two million **pounds** are buried." Because of this, the area is now called the Money Pit.

CHAPTER 2 | 9

They kept **digging**. At 98 feet (30 m) deep, the hole filled with water. They couldn't search any deeper. Was this a **booby trap**? Maybe tunnels connected the pit to the ocean. If so, who dug them? What were they hiding?

In 1849, people drilled with an **auger**. They said they found pieces of a pocket watch. They think they found pieces of a wooden chest, too.

DID YOU KNOW?

Treasure hunting costs a lot of money. Tools are needed. Workers must be paid. Many people run out of money while searching.

10 CHAPTER 2

CHAPTER 2

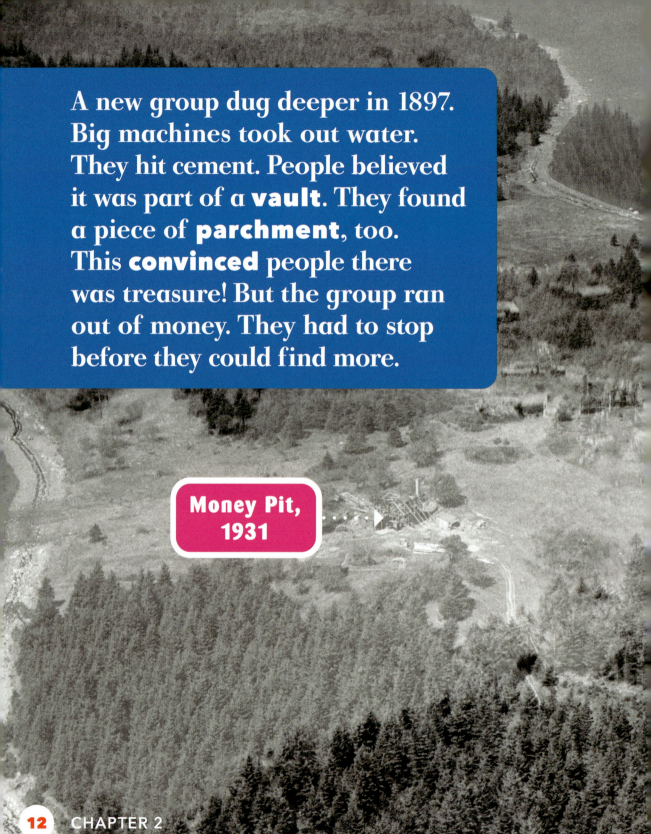

A new group dug deeper in 1897. Big machines took out water. They hit cement. People believed it was part of a **vault**. They found a piece of **parchment**, too. This **convinced** people there was treasure! But the group ran out of money. They had to stop before they could find more.

Money Pit, 1931

TAKE A LOOK!

What are the layers of the Money Pit? What was found in each? Take a look!

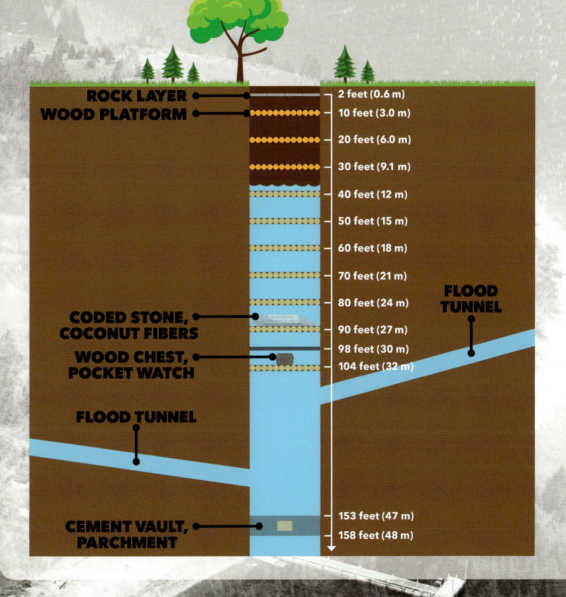

CHAPTER 2

People still search the island. In 2014, a TV show began following the Lagina brothers. They treasure hunt on the island. What do they think is buried? There are many **theories**. Pirates once sailed nearby. Some believe pirates hid treasure here.

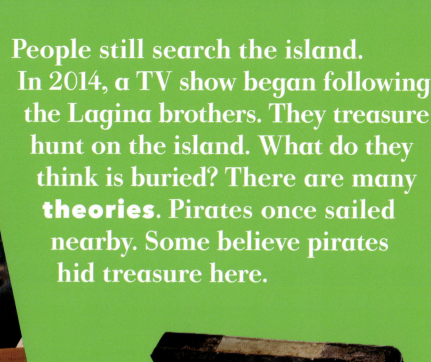

CHAPTER 2   15

Some say it is gold. In the 1500s, Spanish explorers stole gold from **native** peoples. Maybe the explorers stopped at Oak Island. Did they hide the gold here?

WHAT DO YOU THINK?

Imagine you had treasure. What would it be? Where would you hide it?

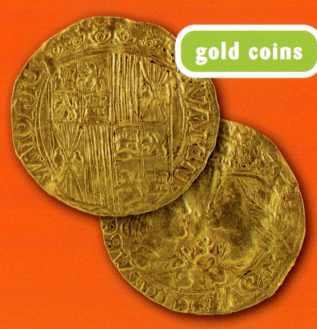

gold coins

16 CHAPTER 2

CHAPTER 2

CHAPTER 3
OTHER THEORIES

Some people believe there is no treasure. The Money Pit could be a **sinkhole**. The water might be ocean water coming through cracks in the earth.

Sailors stopped at the island. Sailors often used coconut fibers to pack items on ships. Maybe that is where the coconut fibers came from.

coconut fibers

CHAPTER 3 19

We may never know if there is treasure on Oak Island. Maybe it was taken long ago. Or maybe one day someone will find something special!

DID YOU KNOW?

Stories say there is a **curse** on the treasure. It says seven people must die before the treasure can be found.

CHAPTER 3

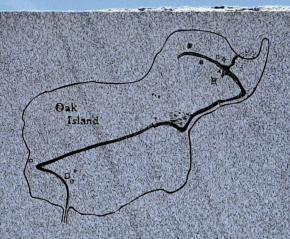

OAK ISLAND MEMORIAL
1795 — 1995

IN MEMORY OF THOSE WHO LOST THEIR LIVES WHILE PURSUING THE OAK ISLAND QUEST

UNKNOWN	1861
MAYNARD KAISER	MAR. 26, 1897
ROBERT RESTALL, Sr	AUG. 17, 1965
ROBERT RESTALL, Jr	AUG. 17, 1965
CYRIL HILTZ	AUG. 17, 1965
CARL GRAESER	AUG. 17, 1965

CHAPTER 3

QUICK FACTS & TOOLS

OAK ISLAND MYSTERY

QUICK FACTS

Location: Oak Island, Nova Scotia, Canada

First Treasure Hunt: 1795

First Treasure Hunters: Daniel McGinnis, John Smith, and Anthony Vaughan

Some Items Found from 1795 to 2014: wooden platforms, coconut fibers, stone with strange carvings, piece of parchment, pocket watch links

GLOSSARY

auger: A tool with a spiral shaft used for drilling holes.

booby trap: A harmless-looking object with a hidden device that tricks a person when it is touched.

code: A system of letters, symbols, or numbers used instead of ordinary words to send messages.

convinced: Persuaded to believe someone or something.

curse: A spell intended to cause harm.

explore: To travel and look around to discover.

fibers: Thin strands of material.

layer: Something above or below something else.

native: A person who was born or lives in a particular place.

parchment: Heavy paperlike material from the skin of animals used for writing on.

platform: A flat structure on which people or objects can stand.

pounds: Units of money used in the United Kingdom.

sinkhole: A hollow place in the ground.

theories: Ideas or opinions that are based on some facts or evidence but are not proven.

vault: A room or compartment for keeping money or valuables safe.

QUICK FACTS & TOOLS   23

INDEX

booby trap 10
chest 10, 13
coconut fibers 8, 13, 19
code 9, 13
curse 20
Lagina brothers 15
McGinnis, Daniel 4, 5, 6
Money Pit 9, 10, 13, 18
Nova Scotia 4
oak tree 5

parchment 12, 13
pirates 15
platform 6, 8, 13
pocket watch 10, 13
sailors 19
sinkhole 18
Spanish explorers 16
treasure 10, 12, 15, 16, 18, 20
vault 12, 13
water 10, 12, 18

TO LEARN MORE

Finding more information is as easy as 1, 2, 3.

❶ **Go to www.factsurfer.com**

❷ **Enter "OakIslandmystery" into the search box.**

❸ **Choose your book to see a list of websites.**